Who are Refugees and Migrants? and Other Big Questions

What makes People Leave their Homes?

Michael Rosen & Annemarie Young

WAYLAND

www.waylandbooks.co.uk

For Emma, Elsie and Emile (M.R.)
In memory of my parents and grandparents, and for all those who have to seek asylum (A.Y.)

First published in Great Britain in 2016 by Wayland

Michael Rosen and Annemarie Young have asserted their rights to be identified as the Author of this Work.

Editor: Nicola Edwards
Design: Rocket Design (East Anglia) Ltd

Artwork by Oli Frape

ISBN: 978 0 7502 9985 5
10 9 8 7 6 5 4 3 2 1

Wayland, an imprint of
Hachette Children's Group
Part of Hodder and Stoughton
Carmelite House
50 Victoria Embankment
London EC4Y 0DZ

An Hachette UK Company
www.hachette.co.uk
www.hachettechildrens.co.uk

Printed and bound in China

We would like to thank:
Muzoon Almellehan, Meltem Avcil, Omid Djalili, Benjamin Zephaniah and Nadia Hassani for sharing their experiences with us.
The Malala Fund for helping us to contact Muzoon.
All those who have contributed to the book in some way.
Our excellent editor, Nicola Edwards, for her invaluable input.

Picture acknowledgements:
All images courtesy of Shutterstock except for: Back cover (left) Courtesy of Goldsmiths, University of London, (right) Anthony Robinson; p5 (clockwise from top left): Omid Djalili, Adam Davies/Malala Fund, Benjamin Zephaniah and Meltem Avcil; p8 Courtesy of Goldsmiths, University of London; p10 Anthony Robinson; p14b Getty Images; p15 David Mbiyu/Demotix/Press Association Images; p16 Adam Davies/Malala Fund; p19t © UNHCR/Mark Henley; p22 Omid Djalili; p21t Getty Images; p26 Ken McKay/ITV/Rex/ Shutterstock; p27 Ted Rosen; p28 Wikimedia Commons; p30 Meltem Avcil; p37 Wikimedia Commons; p38 Wikimedia Commons; p30 Wikimedia Commons; p40 Benjamin Zephaniah

Every attempt has been made to clear copyright. Should there be any inadvertent omission, please apply to the publisher for rectification.

The website addresses (URLs) included in this book were valid at the time of going to press. However, it is possible that contents or addresses may have changed since the publication of this book. No responsibility for any such changes can be accepted by either the author or the Publisher.

CONTENTS

Why do we need this book?

The aim of this book is to get you to think for yourself about the questions we raise. Questions like, 'What makes people leave their homes?' and 'What happens to them/how are they treated when they arrive in a new country?'

Every day on television, on the radio and in the papers, people are talking about 'refugees', 'asylum seekers', 'migrants' and 'immigration'. We see pictures of people crammed onto boats, taking difficult journeys, sometimes dying before they get to where they're headed. We might also hear about people 'stowing away' – hiding in trucks, planes and cars – as they try to escape from where they've been living.

Meanwhile, there are important discussions going on about what should happen to these refugees and migrants, and what the countries that receive them should do about the situation.

Sometimes people talk about these things without understanding very much about them. We'll give you information so that you can form your own opinions.

This book aims to help you understand migration, the movement of people, in all its forms.

How the book works

We'll start with definitions of the words. There are definitions of 'refugee' and 'asylum seeker' under international law that all countries within the United Nations are bound by. We will go on to explore the more general meaning of migration, as well as the meaning of 'migrant'. Then we'll tell you about our own, and others', experiences.

After that, we'll ask these and other questions: Why do people leave their homes? How do they travel and what happens when they arrive? Have people always migrated? What is culture and how do we share it?

We will give you the first fourteen 'articles' of the 1948 Universal Declaration of Human Rights and tell you about the United Nations Refugee Agency, known as the UNHCR (United Nations High Commissioner for Refugees) and its Convention relating to the status of refugees.

You'll be able to read the personal stories of Muzoon Almellehan, Benjamin Zephaniah, Meltem Avcil and Omid Djalili, as well as quotes from many other people – refugees and migrants and those who work with them – and an extract from Benjamin's poem *We Refugees*.

There will be questions for you to think about as you read. And at the end you will have the opportunity to think about what you would do if you were faced with the situations and choices made by refugees and migrants, and to write your own Declaration of Human Rights, using the 'think about' questions as a starting point.

Omid Djalili

Muzoon Almellehan

Meltem Avcil

Benjamin Zephaniah

66 ... asylum seekers are human beings with the same feelings, ambitions and dreams as everyone else. People don't seek asylum unless they have to – leaving home, family and friends and embarking on a journey to the unknown under difficult and dangerous conditions is not easy. I have heard people say asylum seekers are criminal parasites and some even call them 'a threat to our future', but I hope people realise that asylum seekers want to be active, responsible and self-reliant members of society and that demonisation is not helpful. 99

DR MOHAMMAD RAZAI, FROM AFGHANISTAN, NOW A DOCTOR
AND MEDICAL RESEARCHER IN THE UK

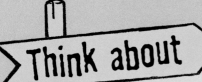
Think about

Do you know where people in your family come from? How far back can you go? Can you put the places they came from next to their names?

Do you know why the people in your family moved? Can you find out?

Who are
refugees and
migrants?

You'll hear and read lots of different terms: 'refugee', 'migrant', 'asylum seeker'. What do these words mean, and what are the differences between them? Does it matter which words we use? There are legal definitions of these words that have been agreed by the United Nations.

> ## Think about
>
> What impressions do you have of how migrants, refugees and asylum seekers are shown on television and in the newspapers?

The United Nations and international law

The United Nations (UN) was established in 1945 straight after the end of the Second World War, in response to the terrible things that had happened during the war, and more immediately, to deal with the huge number of refugees. The aim of the UN is to 'promote international co-operation in order to prevent such conflicts from happening again'. The UN is responsible for international laws that all member states are bound by.

National laws

Individual countries can decide on the details of how they deal with immigrants and asylum seekers, so they each have their own immigration and refugee or asylum laws. But these laws have to respect international law.

The legal definition of a refugee

This is the definition of a refugee from the United Nations Refugee Agency (UNHCR) Convention of 1951:

'A person who owing to a well-founded fear of being persecuted for reasons of race, religion, nationality, membership of a particular social group or political opinion is outside the country of his/her nationality and is unable or, owing to such fear, is unwilling to avail himself/herself of the protection of that country...'

This definition is from the UNHCR website: *'Asylum seeker' describes someone who has applied for protection as a refugee and is waiting to hear if they have been granted refugee status.*

Refugee or migrant? Does it matter which word we use?

Refugees are people who are fleeing armed conflict or persecution, and who would be in danger if forced to return to their own countries. Migrants are people who choose to move not because of a direct threat of persecution or death, but mainly to improve their lives by finding work, or in some cases for education, family reunion, or other reasons. Although those migrants who leave poorer countries would be returning to unemployment and poor conditions, they can, unlike refugees, return home without immediate danger.

So, does it matter if we use the words 'refugee' and 'migrant' interchangeably? Adrian Edwards from UNHCR explains why it does.

"Conflating refugees and migrants can have serious consequences for the lives and safety of refugees. Blurring the two terms takes attention away from the specific legal protections refugees require... We need to treat all human beings with respect and dignity. We need to ensure that the human rights of migrants are respected. At the same time, we also need to provide an appropriate legal response for refugees, because of their particular predicament...

So, at UNHCR we say 'refugees and migrants' when referring to movements of people by sea or in other circumstances where we think both groups may be present... We say 'refugees' when we mean people fleeing war or persecution across an international border. And we say 'migrants' when we mean people moving for reasons not included in the legal definition of a refugee. We hope that others will give thought to doing the same. Choices about words do matter."

A dinghy carrying refugees and migrants reaches the shore of the Greek island of Lesbos.

MY EXPERIENCE

Michael Rosen

I was born in London and I've lived in different parts of London all my life, but many of my older relatives were refugees and migrants. Some left their homes because they were being persecuted. When I look at their stories I can see that, like a lot of families, it's quite complicated, with people travelling to and from the USA and parts of Europe.

My family across the world

My father was born in Massachusetts in the United States of America. He came to England when he was three years old. His father, Morris, travelled from Poland to London when he was a teenager. He met my father's mother, Rose, in London, then together with two boys born in London, they moved to the USA. When things didn't work out between Rose and Morris, Rose came back to England with my father, his sister and baby brother, who were all born in the USA. Morris stayed in the USA with the two boys who had been born in England!

One family, moving between Poland, England and the USA.

Rose was born in Newcastle and her parents were born in Poland. She had a brother and an uncle who moved to South Africa.

On my mother's side, her mother, Annie, was born in what is now Bukovina in Romania. Her father, Frank, was born in England but both his parents were born in Poland.

How I felt

As a boy I always felt special that my dad was American. When my parents talked about Poland, that felt mysterious. But it was also something I didn't tell my friends about because I thought it would make me sound 'foreign', and in the suburbs in the 1950s, that didn't feel safe.

Why all this movement?

All my eight great-grandparents were refugees. They moved from where they lived because of what are called 'pogroms' – a word meaning violent attacks on groups of people. They were attacked because they were Jews.

Back with Morris, my father's father: all his brothers and sisters were born in Poland. One brother went to the USA, two brothers moved to France but were transported to Poland during World War II and were killed in Auschwitz concentration camp. One sister stayed in Poland, and we think she died during the war but we don't know how. Her son, Michael, fled from the invading army into Russia, where he was put in prison. Then he joined the Polish Free Army, travelled with that army through the Middle East, across North Africa into Italy and he ended up in London in the house of my father's sister. He lives in London today.

66 When I look at all this migration, it makes me think that we are citizens of the world, and things can happen that might make us migrate at any time. 99

Think about

What do you think would make you want to leave your home?

England
France
Russia
Poland
USA
Italy
North Africa
Middle East
South Africa

MY EXPERIENCE

Annemarie Young

All four of my grandparents were immigrants or the children of immigrants and so were my parents. My mother's mother and her family moved from St Petersburg to Odessa, in Russia, and then to Alexandria and Cairo in Egypt. Her father and his family moved from Acre in Palestine to Cairo. My father's mother went from Naples in Italy to Cairo, while his father was born in Cairo, son of a Scottish train driver and a Greek mother. And my parents, both born in Cairo, emigrated to Australia in 1949.

I too am an immigrant! I was born in Australia, but left there in my mid twenties and I now live in Cambridge, in the UK.

'But what *are* you?'

When I was a child, growing up in Adelaide, Australia in the 1950s and 1960s, I was often asked 'But what *are* you?'. The other children knew that my family were immigrants, then called 'new Australians'. When they asked me 'Where do your parents come from?' they expected a straightforward answer. But there wasn't one. My parents had come from Egypt; we spoke mostly French at home (that's another story!), but they were neither straightforwardly Egyptian nor French. To further complicate matters, they'd had British passports but were obviously not English. So, indeed, what were they? And what was I? There wasn't a simple answer.

As a child and a teenager, I wasn't very sure of my identity. My simple Scots surname (Young) didn't tell the whole story of my mixed background, so I could often get away with pretending to be an Australian of British heritage. But as soon as my parents came into the picture it was obvious we were not: both my parents looked, and they certainly sounded, foreign. So I was usually made to feel odd and 'other'.

My parents mostly felt welcome and accepted, but at the time there was an underlying wariness of those from other backgrounds, and it wasn't until I was at university that my 'exotic' background became interesting to other people, and I no longer felt embarrassed by it. And then I started to feel that I did not want to stay in Australia after all, so for ten years I travelled and lived in many different places. Eventually I decided that the UK was where I wanted to be, so I came to England for a job and there I've stayed.

People have always been on the move

What has always struck me when I look at the movements of my family is that in those times, borders and nationalities were not so fixed. It wasn't easy to pin people down to only one definition of themselves.

In the nineteenth and early twentieth centuries when my great-grandfather and grandparents arrived there, Egypt was part of the Ottoman Empire and there were people from all over Europe and further afield living there. In those days, people moved countries quite easily, and most did not think of themselves as immigrants. There were fewer restrictions on movements. Some people moved for jobs and others left situations that were difficult – sometimes as a result of poverty, or in other cases they were targeted because of their religion or ethnic background.

Think about

Annemarie talks about not having one definition of herself. Is that anything like you?

66 As a child and a teenager, I wasn't very sure of my identity. 99

What makes people leave their homes?

'What made you leave?'

Do people migrate because there's a strong reason for leaving? Or do people migrate because there's a strong reason for going to a particular place?

Quite often people say that they moved somewhere because they heard that there were jobs, or they heard that they would be free to practise their religion. At first glance, this sounds as though the reason for going somewhere is more important than the reason to leave. But then, if there were good jobs where they lived, or if they were free to practise their religion the way they wanted to, such people wouldn't leave.

Think about

If you lived in a country where there was no health care, not enough schools for everyone, very little chance of going to college, very few jobs, what do you think you would do?

So, the starting point in all migration stories is 'what made you leave?'

Poverty, war or persecution

For some people, it's about weighing up the difference between making a living where they are, or trying to start from scratch somewhere new. The world is a very uneven place. In some places, most people are very poor, there are very few hospitals and doctors; there are very few schools; when you are old there is very little chance that your place of work or the government has saved money for you to provide you with a pension to live on.

People watch television and films and see how others in the world live. If they are poor and hungry, these people might think that there's more chance of a job, more chance to earn some money, in another country that they've heard about from relations or friends, or seen on television.

For many of the refugees in the Middle East, who we see on television, the answer to that question is simple: they don't want to be killed and they don't want people in their family to be killed.

Sometimes it's about 'persecution'. This means being threatened, hunted down, hurt because of who you are, what you believe, what you look like. Or, perhaps, that people think 'your sort' are the wrong sort for some reason.

Persecuted people will often try to run away.

Think about

War is one of the main reasons why people leave their homes and countries. What do you think governments can do or should do about war?

These people at a railway station in Hungary are refugees fleeing war in their home countries.

Mesut Özil

Mesut Özil is an internationally famous footballer who plays for the German national team, and for Arsenal in England. His grandfather was a migrant labourer from Turkey, and he is a practising Muslim. In 2010, Mesut received an award for being a 'prime example of successful integration within German society'.

Describing how he plays football, he says:

"My technique and feeling for the ball is the Turkish side to my game. The discipline, attitude and always-give-your-all is the German part."

Migrant labour

There have been times when countries have discovered that they haven't got enough people to do the work needed to build up the country. Then, people from the government have gone to other countries and said, 'Come to our country. We need you to help build new houses, run the hospitals, drive the trains and buses.'

Passengers arrive at Tilbury Docks in June 1948 after travelling from Jamaica on a ship called the Empire Windrush *to take up jobs in the UK.*

Unaccompanied children

In recent times, something else seems to be happening more than ever before. Young people, aged between eight and sixteen, have been leaving their countries on their own, without their parents or whoever has been looking after them. Sometimes this is because where they are is frightening, sometimes it's because their parents have been killed, sometimes it's because their parents send them off in the hope that they will be safer and happier somewhere else.

Think about

How would you feel if you were separated from your parents or the people who are looking after you? How would you try to find out who was a good person to talk to and who wasn't?

Warsan Shire

Warsan Shire, who was born in Kenya to Somali parents and brought up in London, was appointed the first Young Poet Laureate of London in 2014. She has been writing highly acclaimed poetry since her teens, and has written powerfully about the refugee experience, including the poem *Home*, which you can read online. In 2016, Warsan Shire's name hit the global headlines when Beyoncé featured her poetry in the 'visual album' *Lemonade*.

❝ Nobody in their right mind chooses to risk his or her life and embark on a journey full of danger and the unknown. ... While the political action takes time, it is a humanitarian imperative that all persons who need assistance receive it. **❞**

Marianne Gasser, Head of the International Committee of the Red Cross (ICRC) Delegation in Syria

MY EXPERIENCE

Muzoon Almellehan

Muzoon Almellehan is a Syrian refugee living in the UK. She arrived with her father, mother, two brothers and sister, after living in refugee camps in Jordan for three years. In 2016, Muzoon was invited to speak to world leaders at the Supporting Syria Conference in London. This is what she told them.

What all refugees want is for life to be normal. I hope that with the help of the UK and many other countries, more refugees will be able to have a normal life – especially the children.

I am only one girl, but like all girls, I have dreams.

My dream is to go to university and to be a journalist. When I am a journalist, I want to tell the stories of different people and different countries, so we can work together.

Before the war, we lived in Dara'a in Syria where my father was a teacher. I loved to go to school. But when war came he could not go to work and going to school was too dangerous. Sometimes there was no food. So we went across the border to the Kingdom of Jordan, which gave safety to us and many other families.

In Jordan, we lived in two refugee camps. Life was not easy, but I was lucky because I was in camps where there were schools. I am also lucky because I have parents who believe in education, especially for their daughters.

We need education because Syria needs us. Syria needs engineers and teachers, doctors and journalists. If young people are not educated, who will rebuild the country? Without us, who will build peace?

I share the same message as my friend Malala: Education is power. Education is the future. Education makes us who we want to be.

I said this to world leaders when Malala and I had the chance to speak at an important conference about Syria in London. I said to world leaders: Education was important for you in your life. It is important for your children. It is important for Syrian children, too.

Some people call us the Lost Generation. We are not lost. We have not lost our love of learning. We have not lost our dreams for our future.

We have not lost hope. Syria will never be the same as before the war. I hope it can be better.

One day, when I am a journalist, there is a story I want to write. I want to write the story of how all the Syrian children came home to lift up their country.

I hope that story starts now.

❝ We have not lost our dreams for our future. ❞

Muzoon's campaign for girls' education

Almost three million Syrian children are unable to go to school as a result of the conflict in their country. Before the war, 12 years of education was available to all, but now early marriage rates have risen, along with child labour. Muzoon started campaigning for girls to go to classes while she was living in the refugee camps. When Malala Yousafzai visited Jordan, the two girls became friends. Now in the UK, Muzoon continues her campaign for girls' education with the Malala Fund.

> **Think about**
>
> Do you understand why Muzoon and Malala think going to school is so important? What do you think?

Malala Yousafzai

Malala became the youngest ever recipient of the Nobel Peace Prize for her work in championing the rights of all children to education. She was shot and seriously injured because she spoke out against the Taliban's attempts to stop girls from going to school.

On her 18th birthday in 2015 she visited a refugee camp in Lebanon. She said, "... I have a message for the leaders of this country, this region and the world – you are failing the Syrian people, especially Syria's children. This is a heartbreaking tragedy – the world's worst refugee crisis in decades."

How do refugees and migrants travel?

What happens when they arrive?

How people travel depends on why they are leaving their home countries.

People fleeing conflict, or disasters, often have to leave without much warning; they might have to go on foot, by taxi, minibus, lorries, or by whatever means they can find. If they have little money, they won't have many choices and many can only get as far as crossing the border of their country. Most refugees hope to return soon to their homes, and this is another reason they stay close. The great majority of refugees stay within their own region, and this is why the countries close to those in conflict have the largest numbers of refugees.

Refugees may travel many hundreds of miles over land and sea to reach countries where they have relatives, or where they hope to find communities which will help them. A much smaller number may arrive by plane.

Some refugees use 'people-smugglers' to help them get away. They have to pay the smugglers a great deal of money, and they usually travel in appalling conditions.

Migrants who have made arrangements in advance and have valid visas to go to a particular country usually travel by plane, train or car.

Think about

If using a people-smuggler was the only way for you to get away from war or persecution, what would you do?

What happens to refugees when they leave their home countries?

This varies across the world. In the countries where refugees are found in the greatest numbers, huge refugee camps exist. UNHCR and international aid groups provide shelters and other aid, but life is difficult for the people who live there, and it's especially hard for children. Their schooling is disrupted and it's almost impossible for them to get a proper education.

Aqueela Asisfi

Aqueela Asisfi is a trained teacher who had to flee from Afghanistan in 1993 when the Taliban took over. She now lives and teaches in a refugee camp in Pakistan. She has won an award for her work, and was also shortlisted for the Global Teacher Prize in 2016.

When she arrived as a refugee, there were no schools in the local area. Despite the challenges, Aqueela set up a school in a borrowed tent and worked hard to overcome resistance and negative attitudes. From its small beginnings, her school has produced over 1,000 graduates – most of them Afghan refugee girls, but also local Pakistani children. Some have become doctors, engineers, government officials and teachers in Afghanistan.

Some refugee camps have existed for many years, with children growing up there and then having their own families. One of the oldest camps, Shatila in southern Beirut in Lebanon, was set up in 1949 for displaced Palestinian refugees. It's still there, and those refugees cannot return home. The Dadaab refugee camp complex, in Kenya, is the largest in the world; the first camp there was set up in 1992.

Think about

What do you think would be the most difficult thing about living in a refugee camp?

Children from Syrian refugee families play together at a refugee camp in Turkey.

How are asylum seekers, refugees and migrants welcomed?

OFFICIALLY

People who ask for asylum in European countries are generally entitled to food (or money to buy it), shelter and medical attention, schooling for their children, and access to interpreters and lawyers.

In most countries, asylum seekers are not allowed to work, but they are given a small allowance, or vouchers to buy food. It's only once they have been granted refugee status that they are allowed to work and to live as citizens of that country.

Migrants who have valid visas are usually allowed to work as soon as they arrive. In some countries, like Australia, migrants are given free language lessons.

UNOFFICIALLY

Communities can make asylum seekers and migrants feel welcome or they can make them feel decidedly unwelcome. They can do this in lots of different ways.

Sometimes families and individuals will offer to take refugees into their homes. Many communities have set up centres where refugees can go to meet other people and get support.

Sometimes, there are people who feel threatened by those coming to their country, whether they are refugees or immigrants. They demonstrate against government decisions to take in asylum seekers or migrants, often using racist language.

Think about

In some countries, there are people who have made it clear that they don't want migrants, refugees and asylum seekers to be allowed in and made welcome. What do you think about that?

Australia and the United States

Anyone who arrives in Australia without already having a valid visa is regarded as an 'unlawful non-citizen' and detained. If people arrive by air they will often be granted a 'bridging visa' and allowed to stay while their asylum claim is processed. But this doesn't apply to people who arrive by boat. In fact, Australia has been criticised by the UNHCR for detaining thousands of people – men, women and children – in detention centres outside Australia, and for turning away boats carrying asylum seekers from reaching their shores.

The Australian government provides limited assistance for those asylum seekers who are allowed into the country.

In the United States, asylum seekers who arrive without documents are detained while they are waiting for their claims to be dealt with. Charities provide support, not the government.

A story of welcome

Tindyebwa was adopted by actors Emma Thompson and Greg Wise as a sixteen-year-old refugee from Rwanda. He'd lost his whole family and been press-ganged as a child soldier when he was twelve. He fled to the UK with the help of an aid agency. He's now a human rights lawyer and activist. He says:

TIndyebwa (second from the left) at an awards ceremony with his adoptive parents and sister.

"When you arrive in a new country you have to quickly adapt and accept that you have to learn new things and incorporate your background with the new environment. That's how you survive really. Those who have been most successful have tried to integrate, they've not completely left their background but they've accepted that life has gone on. It has been a long journey, home is always best, but it just happens in a snap when things are difficult and sometimes you are forced to move away. It is a constant learning experience."

Unwelcoming responses

The Bulgarian 'wall'

The government of Bulgaria has put up an 80-kilometre barrier made of razor wire along the country's border with Turkey, to prevent refugees and migrants from entering the country.

Demonstrations against immigrants and refugees in Germany

The German government has been the most generous and welcoming in Europe. This has led to some demonstrations against the government, by nationalist movements and other extremists who are against anyone who they consider as outsiders and who have a different culture.

Counter demonstrators gather in Germany to show their support for refugees and their disagreement with those who have protested against them.

Omid Djalili

Omid Djalili is a British–born Iranian comedian and actor. He has performed on television and in films, including *The Mummy*, *Gladiator* and *Shaun the Sheep The Movie*. He is a huge football fan and still hopes to get spotted by one of the big Premier League clubs ...

Why did we leave Iran?

My parents left Iran in 1957, and always intended to go back, but in 1979, the Islamic revolution occurred which made returning impossible. My father lost his job at the Iranian Embassy and for a time we had refugee status in the UK, before eventually gaining citizenship. Many of my parents' friends in Iran suffered terribly during those years and it had a big effect on the atmosphere in our home.

We were Bahá'ís, a religion that was and still is being persecuted in Iran. Many are unjustly imprisoned, lose their livelihoods and property, and even today young Bahá'ís are often denied the rights to attend schools and universities.

66 I think we are all affected when one part of humanity suffers. 99

What it was like living in London

My mother was a dressmaker and felt lucky to live in London, a city of culture and fashion. Although my parents mostly socialised with fellow Iranians, they felt great appreciation for the British people they met, all of whom were kind.

At school I felt embarrassed for a while by my Iranian identity because the images on the BBC news were of religious fanatics behaving in extreme ways. This felt so opposite to all the Iranians I knew, who were warm and hospitable. I even tried to pretend I was Italian for a while and told people that my name was Chico. Unfortunately this didn't catch on.

I sometimes felt embarrassed by my parents because their English was not so great in the beginning. They were both physically affectionate and expressive, which contrasted with the reserve of English people, especially my teachers at school. I remember being very embarrassed once when my mother started sobbing with happiness and tried to hug my drama teacher who had said some encouraging words about me at a parents' meeting.

Friends not strangers

I regard myself now as British but I am proud of my Iranian roots. One of my spiritual beliefs is that the Earth is One Country and Humankind its Citizens. I'm very affected by the current plight of the migrants and refugees. I have been extremely fortunate to make my home in London, and I think we are all affected when one part of humanity suffers. I hope that I will live to see the day when we regard each other as friends not strangers, and care for each other as part of one human family.

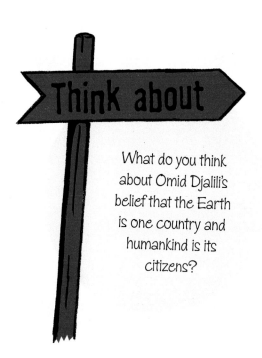

Think about

What do you think about Omid Djalili's belief that the Earth is one country and humankind is its citizens?

Migrations
through history

How far back does migration go?

The word 'migration' comes from a Latin word meaning 'to move about' and it was first used in English in the early seventeenth century, to talk about people moving.

Migration describes what human beings have been doing for as long as there have been humans. Our reasons for moving, though, may be very different.

Migration driven by the search for food, conquest and empire, and the slave trade

It's thought that many of the 'native' or 'first nation' peoples of North America originally came from what is now northern Russia. They would have moved following herds of animals and looking for places to settle. That's migration of peoples looking for or following food.

For a while, in the British Isles, the Romans ruled. That's because Roman soldiers and their governor from Rome (in what is now Italy) invaded and defeated the people living in Britain. That's migration through conquest and empire.

Millions of people were taken from Africa and made to work in South, Central and North America and the Caribbean. This was migration because of slavery.

This photograph shows several generations of a family of slaves, who were all born on the same plantation.

Migration through war, famine and transportation

At the end of the Second World War, there were millions of people who found that their homes had been destroyed, or they had fled from battles and didn't want to go back to the countries they used to live in. Others had been taken to prisons, camps or forced labour factories. All these were called 'displaced' people and millions ended up living somewhere new. This is migration through war.

Another famous migration is when millions of Irish people moved to the United States because of famine in Ireland in the middle of the nineteenth century.

The reason why many Australians have British or Irish names is because their ancestors came from Britain and Ireland. Many of them were taken there as 'convicts' in what was called 'transportation'. It was a punishment for what were sometimes small crimes, but there were also Irish political prisoners and serious criminals amongst the convicts.

Think about

Do you know of any other major migrations not mentioned here?

Gulwali Passarlay

Acclaimed writer Gulwali Passarlay was a refugee from Afghanistan. When he was 12 years old, he and his elder brother were sent away by their mother because they were in danger from the Taliban. Gulwali had a harrowing journey; he suffered great hardship and nearly died. When he arrived in the UK, the border authorities did not believe his age or his story, and he spent a difficult time worrying that he might be deported. Eventually, Gulwali gained asylum.

He's now written a book, *The Lightless Sky*, and he says: "I have been changed forever by what I have witnessed. But after all my awful experiences, I don't want to waste a single second. I came here and I want to make a difference. I don't just take. I give back."

When are we 'strangers'?

These quotes from William Shakespeare and Barack Obama help us to reflect on this question.

The Shakespeare quote is taken from something that he wrote about a speech Sir Thomas More made at a time (the May Day riots of 1517) when there were anti-immigrant riots against the French Protestants who were seeking asylum in London. He refers to the immigrants as 'strangers'. He's asking people to imagine what it would be like if they were sent away from England by the King, and they went to Europe to seek refuge. Then they too would be strangers.

Sir Thomas More:

"You'll put down strangers,/ Kill them, cut their throats, possess their houses... Alas, alas! Say now the King... banish you: whither would you go?/What country, by the nature of your error,/ Should give you harbour? Go you to France or Flanders,/ To any German province, Spain or Portugal,/ Nay, anywhere that not adheres to England:/ Why, you must needs be strangers."

Speaking almost 400 years after Shakespeare's death, President Obama used the same word to describe migrants:

President Barack Obama:

"My fellow Americans, we are and always will be a nation of immigrants. We were strangers once, too. And whether our forebears were strangers who crossed the Atlantic, or the Pacific, or the Rio Grande, we are here only because this country welcomed them in, and taught them that to be an American is about something more than what we look like, or what our last names are, or how we worship. What makes us Americans is our shared commitment to an ideal – that all of us are created equal, and all of us have the chance to make of our lives what we will."

Mo Farah

Mo Farah was born in Somalia and came to the UK at the age of eight. He is the UK's most successful runner, having won gold medals at the 2012 London Olympics for the 5,000 and 10,000 metres races. He says he is proud to be an immigrant living in Britain.

"I don't really remember too much about Somalia as I was so young. But me and my family felt so at home in the UK because the people are so welcoming, it is a truly multi-cultural society. I am proud of my dual heritage and proud to be British. When I run, I run for Great Britain."

Migration as a response to disaster, trade and jobs

Sometimes people flee volcanoes, earthquakes and floods. One example is the devastation caused when the volcano on the Caribbean island of Montserrat erupted in 1995. Two-thirds of the population were evacuated, many came to the UK and most have not returned.

Sometimes people are invited to go somewhere where there are jobs, or where there are jobs that seem better.

Some people move because they find that that's the best way to 'trade' – to buy and sell things.

Nadia Hassani

Nadia Hassani's father was an immigrant to Germany, where she was born and grew up. She emigrated from there to the United States as an adult. She is a translator and is also the author of a cookbook, *Spoonfuls of Germany*, and several blogs. She says:

"When I was growing up, I wasn't a migrant myself, I was half-and-half – my mother was from Germany and my father was an immigrant from Tunisia. He came to Germany in the early 1960s and I was born there. My father completely assimilated and barely conveyed any of his culture to me. I grew up like a German, and as a child and teenager I felt like I was not at all different from any of my peers. But in the eyes of the world around me, I was different. My Arab name and looks gave me away as not being 'genuinely' German and I was singled out as alien, often asked where I was from, and spoken to in broken, primitive German. That made me unhappy and uncomfortable. Based on my experience I can only imagine how real migrants must feel in a new country. But Germany was a different country back then, much less diverse than it is today, where 20 per cent of the population has a migration background."

What is the situation now?

The reason why there is a 'crisis' now, is mostly because of war. It may seem obvious, but most people don't like war and they run away from it. The problem with that is that we live in countries or 'nation states' and for political reasons, the leaders of nation states tend to say, 'We look after the people in our country first'.

This means that the modern story of migration is not only about the movement of people, it's about the borders and frontiers of countries; who's allowed to cross and who isn't.

What rights do refugees and migrants have?

Because of the horrors of the Second World War, the United Nations agreed to draw up a set of basic principles. The Universal Declaration of Human Rights is one of the most significant and far reaching statements to be agreed on by all the major countries of the world. It sets out the fundamental rights of all people, and one of the articles relates specifically to those seeking asylum from persecution in any form.

The Universal Declaration of Human Rights

The extracts on page 29 are taken from the Universal Declaration of Human Rights. They are the main details from the 'preamble' (introduction) and the first 14 of the 30 'articles', as they are called. The last one refers directly to asylum from persecution. The Declaration was drafted by representatives from all regions of the world, and proclaimed by the United Nations General Assembly in Paris on 10 December, 1948.

German refugees who lost their homes during the Second World War gather with their few belongings at a railway station in Berlin in 1945.

Preamble

The Preamble states "Whereas recognition of the inherent dignity and of the equal and inalienable rights of all members of the human family is the foundation of freedom, justice and peace in the world ...

... it is essential ... that human rights should be protected by the rule of law."

These are extracts from the Universal Declaration of Human Rights:

Article 1
All human beings are born free and equal in dignity and rights.

Article 2
Everyone is entitled to all the rights and freedoms set forth in this Declaration, without distinction of any kind, such as race, colour, sex, language, religion, political or other opinion, national or social origin, property, birth or other status.

Article 3
Everyone has the right to life, liberty and security of person.

Article 4
No one shall be held in slavery or servitude; slavery and the slave trade shall be prohibited in all their forms.

Article 5
No one shall be subjected to torture or to cruel, inhuman or degrading treatment or punishment.

Article 6
Everyone has the right to recognition everywhere as a person before the law.

Article 7
All are equal before the law and are entitled without any discrimination to equal protection of the law.

Article 8
Everyone has the right to an effective remedy by the competent national tribunals for acts violating the fundamental rights ...

Article 9
No one shall be subjected to arbitrary arrest, detention or exile.

Article 10
Everyone is entitled in full equality to a fair and public hearing by an independent and impartial tribunal.

Article 11
(1) Everyone charged with a penal offence has the right to be presumed innocent until proved guilty according to law in a public trial at which he or she has had all the guarantees necessary for his or her defence.

Article 12
No one shall be subjected to arbitrary interference with ... privacy, family, home or correspondence, nor to attacks upon ... honour and reputation.

Article 13
(1) Everyone has the right to freedom of movement and residence within the borders of each state.

(2) Everyone has the right to leave any country, including their own, and to return to their country.

Article 14
(1) Everyone has the right to seek and to enjoy in other countries asylum from persecution.

UNHCR statement on refugees

"Grounded in Article 14 of the Universal Declaration of human rights, which recognizes the right of persons to seek asylum from persecution in other countries, the United Nations Convention relating to the Status of Refugees, adopted in 1951, is the centrepiece of international refugee protection today."

Think about

Imagine you are in charge of all migration into your country. What kinds of things would you do to fit in with what the United Nations agreed in 1951 that all nations should do?

MY EXPERIENCE

Meltem Avcil

Meltem and her mother came to England from Turkey when Meltem was seven years old. Her family are Kurdish. The situation for Kurds is complex and her village was targeted by Turkish soldiers. After many difficulties, including two stints at Yarl's Wood detention centre, Meltem is now a multi-award-winning activist, campaigning against detention for refugee women and children.

Why did we leave?

Not fitting in is common amongst children, but it's even more common among adults. The adults we look up to fight for land, religion, politics and most of all, money. Unfortunately for my family, we were stuck in the middle of an illogical war. A chaos called war. We had to leave for a better homeland.

What was it like when we got here?

When I first arrived, I wondered 'why are these people so white and yellow?' I didn't know blonde back when I was seven years old. Though I never felt left out, not knowing the language always got in the way of fitting in and expressing myself. As asylum seekers, we were constantly moved. From Bradford to Doncaster to London to Bedford to Kent to Newcastle and finally back to London.

We suffered from racism in Bradford, with smashed windows and threats, and the empty house next door was set on fire. So we were sent to Doncaster, which was good, it felt normal. I had friends, went to school and had fun. I learned English in three months there. But then our troubles started again and we went to London to stay with my aunt, then back to Doncaster again and more normality for another few years.

The worst was when five security guards stormed into our house and took us to Yarl's Wood detention centre. We got out the first time, but a year later we were taken back to Yarl's Wood after we were told that our asylum application had been rejected and we would be deported. Yarl's Wood was frightening and depressing. We were there for three months. We were taken to the airport to be deported and two guards took us onto the plane, but I started screaming and shouting and they took us off. Then something magic happened and the Children's Commissioner got us out of detention. We finally got asylum.

I've had many accents throughout my life

My accents have varied from Yorkshire to Geordie, and now I have a London accent. I met with so many accents and places as a kid that now everything seems possible. Because of the constant movement, I had the silly impression that people ruled my life to the point where I used to ask my mum if I could use the bathroom at my own temporary home.

I stayed here because this is my home

I had met a lot of people and places. Even though I was locked up at the age of 13 for three months in a detention centre, I knew I could not return to a strange land because by this time I felt at home in England. So I started a campaign against keeping women and children in detention and it ended up helping many lives as well as mine.

> **Think about** >

Do you know anyone who is a migrant, refugee or asylum seeker?

Have you been surprised to find out that someone has that kind of background?

I believed I could make a difference

Now I am a twenty-two year-old activist, a student of psychology and a writer. All because I believed I could do it and that good was on my side. The wars in the world right at this moment are driving millions of people like me to flee, and hundreds to die in cold seas. So either way, it's death for many people. If we carry on destroying land and people, then where do we end up?

Do not allow others to label you. Because once you are labelled as anything, it is hard to break away. Be yourself, and the world can be your best friend.

> 66 If we carry on destroying land and people, then where do we end up? 99

Does it matter how we use words?

How are words 'suggestive'?

'Suggestive' is when we don't say things directly. Here is a direct statement: 'We don't want strangers here.' Here is someone being suggestive about the same thing: 'You know, some might say that we are happier with people we know.'

Margaret Thatcher

Here is part of a famous speech that Margaret Thatcher, once Prime Minister of Britain, gave in 1978, where she is being 'suggestive'. "There was a committee which ... said that if we went on as we are, then by the end of the century there would be four million people of the new Commonwealth or Pakistan here. Now, that is an awful lot and I think it means that people are really rather afraid that this country might be rather swamped by people with a different culture ..."

'Swamped' – what does this word suggest?

In the passage, you can see the word 'swamped'. 'Swamped' is a word that means overwhelmed. Sometimes people use it to talk about a field that might be swamped because so much water has flooded into it. If you use it about people, it suggests that people migrating are like a flood which covers over or drowns people living somewhere. This is 'suggestive' because it doesn't describe what actually happens when people migrate into a country. No one really gets 'swamped'.

'Us' and 'the other'

When we talk about the people of the world, it's easy to talk as if there's always an 'us' and 'them', or even an 'us' and 'others'. Some commentators said that this is what Mrs. Thatcher did in this speech.

Look at this: "...people (1) are really rather afraid that this country might be rather swamped by people (2) with a different culture." The second 'people' means one group, not the whole people. The first 'people' seems to mean everyone. But it can't be everyone because it doesn't include the people with a different culture. It suggests that there is an 'us' people and a 'them' people without actually saying who is 'us', and who might be 'afraid'.

How do these words make people feel?

Whenever politicians on television and the radio or in newspapers, or in this book, talk about migrants, they might 'suggest' things. You will hear phrases like a 'bunch of migrants' or 'floods' or 'swarms' of migrants.

If you are not a migrant, you can ask yourself whether these words help you to think of migrants as the same as you, better than you or worse than you. If you are a migrant, or your parents are migrants, then you can ask yourself whether words like these make you feel as if you are the same, better or worse than the people using those words.

Rita Ora

Rita Ora is a singer and actress. She was born in Pristina in what is now Kosovo. Her family was forced to flee the country when she was just one year old. Rita and her family arrived in London as refugees. She has said:

66 That word [refugee] carries a lot of prejudice, but it also made us determined to survive. 99

Think about

Why do you think Rita Ora says that the word 'refugee' carries a lot of prejudice?

Ordinary words can change and carry prejudice. Can you think of other words like this?

What is culture and how do we share it?

What is culture?

One word that often comes up when people talk about migration and immigration is 'culture'. People usually mean something like 'how we do things'. This means you could talk about, say, the food you eat, the clothes you wear, the music you enjoy, the jokes that make you laugh, the books you like, as your 'culture'.

Now imagine how, if you were a Martian and you were journeying quickly round the world, you might notice some other things to do with 'how they do things', like: different ways of running a country, different ways of travelling about, different languages, different kinds of houses and apartments. You might also notice things that are very similar: phones, computers, jeans, t-shirts, some fizzy drinks and so on.

One way to describe how we live alongside each other doing different things is to call it 'multicultural'. This suggests that we live in a country or a society of many cultures. Most countries in the world have always been multicultural, where rich and poor, men and women, old and young, new arrivals and longstanding inhabitants, in each of their different ways, express their cultures.

That's one way of looking at it.

How we share cultures

You can turn that around, and look at things we say 'belong' to one culture but when we look closely, it turns out that they come from several cultures. This idea is called 'interculturalism' meaning 'how we share cultures'.

William Shakespeare is sometimes described as a great English or British writer. Fair enough, he was born and lived in Britain and English was his language.

He wrote plays and poems, but when we look at these, we discover that he got many ideas and many of his ways of writing from different places, such as Ancient  Greece and Rome, the Italy of his own day, and the Bible — which came from what we now call the Middle East. One of his most famous plays, *Romeo and Juliet* was first told as an Italian story and Shakespeare adapted it for his play.

Maya Angelou

"Shakespeare must be a black girl."

African American poet Maya Angelou explained that as a young girl she read Shakespeare's Sonnet 29, with its opening lines "When, in disgrace with fortune and men's eyes, I all alone beweep my outcast state", and she thought that the author must have been a black girl because it expressed so clearly what she felt as "an outcast, the victim of racism, destitution, and childhood sexual abuse, crying out alone before a deaf heaven".

Maya Angelou reads her poem On the Pulse of Morning *at the ceremony to mark the beginning of Bill Clinton's presidency in 1993.*

Food, music and clothes

Nearly everyone in Europe eats potatoes and tomatoes at some time in their lives. Potatoes and tomatoes were brought to Europe from South America.

What about music? Nearly all the music we hear in the charts is based on a mix of many musics, especially the 'blues', 'mountain music' and 'gospel'. The 'blues' was a music invented sometime around 1900 by the descendants of African American slaves. Mountain music was invented by the descendants of Irish, Scots and English immigrants to the Appalachian Mountains. Gospel Music was made up out of the hymns of British migrants to the USA mixed in with musical sounds from African Americans.

And clothes: the world's most popular garment is jeans made of a cloth called 'denim'. The first jeans were made by Jacob W. Davis and Levi Strauss in 1853. They were Jewish immigrants from Europe into the USA, but the word 'denim' comes from 'de Nîmes' meaning 'from the town of Nîmes' in France and the word 'jeans' probably comes the Italian town of Genoa.

Think about

Can you think of any music, clothes or food that you like which comes originally from somewhere else?

Inventions, flowers and animals

If you think of all the things we use like electricity, or tar for roads, building materials, cars, trains, planes, computers, phones, and the like – these were invented in many countries, and are nearly all made from or with materials from all over the world, and designed by people from many countries.

Even the flowers, animals and landscapes we look at have been changed by people from many countries. We might say that an area is typically English and then we discover that Dutch engineers drained it. A huge number of garden plants, bushes and trees in British gardens come from all over the world, and animals like grey squirrels and pheasants are 'immigrants'! In recent years, parrots, mink and wallabies have escaped out of captivity and now live here.

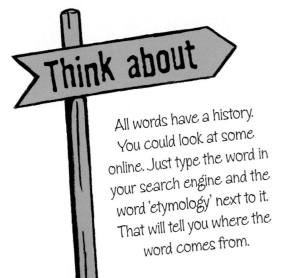

Think about

All words have a history. You could look at some online. Just type the word in your search engine and the word 'etymology' next to it. That will tell you where the word comes from.

Language

And the most famous mixture of all is our language. The main grammar of the English language comes from the tribes of people who lived in what is now Holland, Belgium and Germany. Some key parts of the language come from what is now Denmark, Norway and Sweden. Another big contributor came from the Norman French, most of which originally came from Latin. There are also hundreds of words that come from languages from all over the world.

English is, in a way, the best example of interculturalism of all.

Some English words borrowed from other cultures

crag – Celtic

bread – Anglo-Saxon

take – Danish (Viking)

beauty – French

robot – Czech

coo-ee! – Australian Aboriginal

blitz – German

hey presto! – Italian

jumbo – Swahili

ketchup – Malay and Chinese

pyjamas, cot, jungle, bangle – Hindi

... and there are lots of others too!

What happens when we deliberately separate cultures and people?

At different times in different countries, politicians and leaders have tried to separate cultures and peoples. They've passed laws about it.

Segregation in the Southern States of the United States of America

In the Southern States of the USA, between 1890 and 1965, there were laws separating (or 'segregating', as it was called) white people and African Americans. This meant that people who were described as being of these two 'races' were not allowed to share the same schools, public spaces, buses, trams, trains, public toilets, restaurants, cafes and drinking fountains. The facilities that were provided for African Americans weren't anywhere near the same standard as those for white people. This is known as 'discrimination'. African Americans suffered violence and persecution too.

Many people took big risks to oppose segregation. One of the most famous was Ruby Bridges in New Orleans. When she was six years old, on 14 November, 1960, she was the first African American child to go to a school that had been up until that moment, all-white. At first, all the pupils refused to go to class with her and Ruby had to be protected from angry people shouting at her as she walked into school (see the photograph below). All the teachers apart from one wouldn't teach her, but one, Mrs Henry, taught Ruby all on her own and in the end the school became 'integrated' and other African American children joined the school too.

66 Each and every one of us is born with a clean heart. Our babies know nothing about hate or racism. But soon they begin to learn – and only from us. We keep racism alive. We pass it on to our children. We owe it to our children to help them keep their clean start. 99

RUBY BRIDGES

Nazi Germany

From 1933 to 1945 in Germany, the Nazi Party was in power and they thought that it was a good idea to segregate people. They also passed laws which, they said, would help them make a 'pure' German culture. This meant things like banning music by Jewish composers from the radio, stopping people listening to jazz which they said came from Jews and African Americans, and removing paintings by Jewish artists from public galleries. They even banned paintings by non-Jews which they said had been 'corrupted' by Jewish art.

After the Second World War it was discovered that some Nazis had stolen this art and were enjoying looking at it in private, and that many people loved listening in secret to great jazz by people like Fats Waller and Benny Goodman.

The Nazis also persecuted, imprisoned and exterminated millions of people, trying to wipe out all the Jews and Gypsies. Anyone who didn't fit their definition of an ideal person could be sent to a camp and worked to death or left to die of disease.

These children were photographed at the end of the Second World War.
They had been imprisoned by the Nazis at Auschwitz concentration camp.

Apartheid in South Africa

In South Africa, from 1948 to 1994, there used to be a system of running the country called 'apartheid', which means 'separateness'. Everyone was told which 'race' they belonged to and no one was allowed to marry someone from another 'race'. The government did all it could to make sure that the different races lived apart and that no one should share anything cultural. It wasn't simply a separation, though. Non-whites were discriminated against in many different ways, whether that was because their housing, education and healthcare were bad, or because their conditions of work were awful too.

Any books or films that spoke out against this were banned. One book that was banned was a children's book, *Journey to Jo'burg* by Beverley Naidoo. Beverley couldn't live in South Africa because she had married someone who the government said was of another race. The book was published in Britain and when copies were sent to South Africa, they were seized by customs officers and not allowed to be read by anyone there.

After a long struggle, all the apartheid laws came to an end.

One of the apartheid laws required black South Africans to carry pass books which restricted their travel. In this 1952 photograph, Nelson Mandela burns his pass book in protest.

Think about

Do you know any examples of discrimination?

If you lived in a country where you couldn't go to school because of your religion or because of the colour of your skin, what do you think you would do?

MY EXPERIENCE

Benjamin Zephaniah

Benjamin Zephaniah is a poet, novelist, playwright, musician, performer and television and radio presenter. He's also patron of a number of charities and organisations.

If I talk to anybody for long enough I find that their family came here from somewhere. Everyone comes from somewhere.

My parents came from Jamaica and Barbados

My mum came from Jamaica and my dad came from Barbados, and they met in England. What happened with my mum was that she and her sister were looking at a poster where it said, 'Come to the Motherland ... help build the Mother Country' – that was Britain – and Mum said to her sister, "Fancy going?" and her sister said, "I've heard it's really cold," and Mum said, "Give it a try!" so she did, but her sister stayed behind in Saint Elizabeth. Mum's uncle, who had brought her up, gave her

£20 for the ticket and she came to Britain in 1957.

When I go to Jamaica I see how different people live. Their lives are hard. My cousins are always dying at sea, or in hurricanes, and my family live in poverty, so I'm so aware that if my mum hadn't decided to come to England on that day in 1957, I too would have a difficult life.

My mum always tried to see the nice side of people

Mum said that this country gave her everything. When I took her back to visit Jamaica, she didn't like it, and she wasn't like some Jamaicans who want to go back there to be buried. She wanted to be buried in Witton, in Birmingham.

> **66** When I think about refugees, I think that what they're going through could happen to anyone. **99**

She was like that, but she knew that I was on the receiving end of racist attacks, like when someone slapped a brick on the back of my head. She just didn't like anyone making a fuss about that sort of thing. She'd say, 'We're guests.' And she believed that it would all be all right in the end when we get to heaven. She always tried to see the nice side of people.

People of different backgrounds live together naturally, but when a small thing goes wrong it becomes big news. No one reports it when it goes well, it's not news then. I love our differences. It teaches me that I am a citizen of Britain, but it also teaches me to be a citizen of the world.

Think about

People sometimes talk about 'integration' as though it's only the minority group that integrates with the majority, but have you ever noticed whether people who live, work or go to school with migrants pick up aspects of their culture?

It can happen to anyone

When I think about refugees, I think that what they're going through could happen to anyone. It could happen because of war, or the weather.

I took in some refugees. They were middle class white people from the Lake District in England. They had to grab what they could when the floods came. I think to start off with, they weren't particularly sympathetic to refugees, but they soon changed their mind, because now they know it can happen to anyone.

I wrote a poem called *We Refugees*.

From *We Refugees*

We can all be refugees
Nobody is safe,
All it takes is a mad leader
Or no rain to bring forth food,
We can all be refugees
We can all be told to go,
We can be hated by someone
For being someone.
...
We can all be refugees
Sometimes it only takes a day,
Sometimes it only takes a handshake
Or a paper that is signed.
...
We all came from refugees
Nobody simply just appeared,
Nobody's here without a struggle,
And why should we live in fear
Of the weather or the troubles?
We all came here from somewhere.

What would
you do?

Imagine you are faced with this situation. Soldiers who had threatened to kill your mother or your father are coming to get them. And your family has only one hour to decide what to do.

Who should flee – the whole family? Or should you leave anyone behind? What about the baby, or your grandmother? What should you take with you? Where should you go?

Think about how you'd feel. You are part of this family, and have hardly any time to make these difficult decisions. And what is it like when you arrive in the country you've run to?

To help you think about what it must be like to find yourself in a situation that has become dangerous for your family, we're going to give you a background story, and then ask you to make some decisions about what to do. You might like to try talking these through with a group of your friends.

Background to the situation

Dad is a journalist on the local newspaper. Mum works in the offices of the education authority. They have a baby at home and a boy and a girl at school. Granny lives with them. Uncle Ali, your mum's brother, was a political prisoner for a number of years. He walks with difficulty since he came out of prison. Mum and Dad have an old car. Dad has been a leader of the local journalists trade union.

The situation in the country is getting worse and worse, because:

Two months ago
The army took over the government. Tanks and armoured cars were everywhere. Many people were killed and others arrested. The military rulers have taken over the TV and radio. They've closed down the Internet and have blocked mobile phone signals. Nobody knows what is really going on.

One month ago

Dad was told the new government had arrested certain people. Others, including politicians, writers and trade unionists, have simply 'gone missing'.

An article appeared in a local newspaper. Under a drawing of a skull and coffin was a list of people called 'enemies of the state'. Dad and Uncle Ali were on this list.

Three days ago

A note came through the door. It said Dad was 'a spy and an enemy agent' and that 'his days were numbered'. There was a drawing of a coffin and a skull, a noose and a gun. It was signed 'Friends of the Motherland'.

Two days ago

Someone rang Uncle Ali and told him to get out: some people were planning to set the house on fire.

Yesterday

Some children at school said that squads of soldiers had been searching the streets in a nearby neighbourhood and arresting people, including members of Dad's trade union and people from Mum's office.

Today

The family meets for a hurried discussion. What should you do?

Dad says he and Uncle Ali should flee, and seek political asylum abroad as refugees. Mum says the whole family should go. Who should it be?

How will you travel?

It is under an hour to the border by car, but that journey would be very risky. On foot would mean a whole week's journey through the desert and then the high forest across dangerous country to the frontier.

What should you take with you?

Make a list of the ten most important things to get you to the border of a new country so that you can ask for asylum.

Now

You can hear that the soldiers are starting to search your street. You have ten minutes to make up your minds, get organised and get out – to flee.

When you arrive at your destination country

What do you tell the border patrol or immigration officer? You have lost your documents en route. They will ask you for some sort of proof or evidence for your story. What will you tell them?

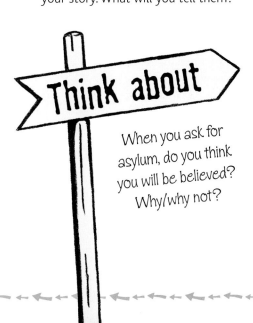

Think about

When you ask for asylum, do you think you will be believed? Why/why not?

What do you think?

The main aim of this book is to get you to think for yourself about the questions we have raised and the information we have given you. Now that you have thought about all the questions and information, try to write a list of human rights that you think everyone should share.

Your own Declaration of Human Rights

The first 'article' of the Universal Declaration of Human Rights says that "All human beings are born free and equal in dignity and rights." The second says that "Everyone is entitled to all the rights and freedoms set forth in this Declaration, without distinction of any kind, such as race, colour, sex, language, religion, political or other opinion, national or social origin, property, birth or other status."

Do you agree with these statements? What would you like to add to make your own declaration about how human beings should treat each other and live together in the world?

Omid Djalili says he believes that 'the earth is one country and humankind is its citizens'. What would you say is your belief about the world and your place in it?

To help you, here are some of the 'Think about' and other questions.

→ Imagine you are in charge of all migration into your country. What kinds of things would you do to fit in with what the United Nations agreed in 1951 that all nations should do?

→ If you lived in a country where there was no healthcare, not enough schools for everyone, very little chance of going to college, very few jobs, what do you think you would do if you were in charge?

→ What do you think about the way migrants, refugees and asylum seekers are shown on television and in the newspapers?

→ War is one of the main reasons why people leave their homes and countries. What do you think governments can do or should do about war?

- Some migrants would love to go back to their country of origin but they don't dare. Do you think you would risk it?

- Do you understand why Muzoon and Malala think going to school is so important?

- In some countries, there are people who have made it clear that they don't want migrants, refugees and asylum seekers to be allowed in and made welcome. What do you think about that?

- Is it possible to say that countries belong to one particular group of people only?

- Do you know any examples of discrimination? If you lived in a country where you were discriminated against, what do you think you would do?

- If you couldn't go to school because of your religion or because of the colour of your skin, what do you think you would do?

- Some of the people in this book have talked about wanting to give something back to the country that has received them. If you were in that situation, what would you do to 'give back'?

Other kinds of migration

It's not only people who migrate. There are other kinds of migration too, and these often cause people to move.

For example, the movement of money – which knows no national borders – is a kind of migration. Those who are in charge of large sums of money, like banks, or people who own large amounts of money themselves, can move money to many places in the world. These movements of money can result in a lack of resources in the place where the money has moved from, which then results in people wanting to move, to emigrate.

Another example is war. War often involves the movement of large amounts of armaments and bombs. As we have seen, wars result in large numbers of refugees as people flee from the danger zones.

> **Think about**

Do you think it's fair to restrict migration of people while the migration of money and bombs is allowed?

GLOSSARY

emigrate When a person leaves their own country in order to settle permanently in another, e.g. *She emigrated from Poland during the Second World War.*

immigrant A person who comes to live permanently in a foreign country, e.g. *She was an immigrant to Scotland.*

migrant A person who moves from one place to another in order to find work or better living conditions. This word also refers to birds and animals that migrate across territories.

refugee A person who is fleeing persecution or armed conflict (see page 6 for the legal definition).

aid agency an organisation that provides aid or support to people in need, particularly international aid

arbitrary describes a decision not based on any reason or system

asylum shelter or protection from danger

charter a written constitution or description of an organisation's functions

citizenship the status of being legally recognised as a national of a state (country)

conflating combining two or more sets of ideas into one

convention an agreement between states (countries)

declaration a written announcement of the terms of an agreement

demonisation the portrayal of something as wicked and threatening

discrimination the unjust treatment of different categories of people, especially on the grounds of race, age, or sex

entitled believing yourself to be deserving of privileges or special treatment

etymology the study of the origin of words and the way in which their meanings have changed

humanitarian concerned with or seeking to promote human welfare

impartial treating everyone involved equally

integration when different cultures come together and share aspects of each other's culture, but at the same time maintain their own identities

interchangeably exchanging one for the other

Nobel Peace Prize – award by a Norwegian committee each year to a person or persons who have done the best work for the promotion of peace in the world

Ottoman Empire an empire that ruled over parts of south eastern Europe and Egypt in the nineteenth and early twentieth centuries

parasites organisms which live in or on another organism and benefit at the other's expense

penal describes a serious offence punishable by law

persecution ill treatment, especially because of race, political or religious beliefs, or sexual orientation

political prisoners people imprisoned because of their political beliefs or actions

prejudice an opinion that is not based on reason or actual experience

press-ganged forcibly enlisted into the army or navy

proclaim to make an official announcement

protocol the original draft of a document setting out the terms of an agreement

refugee camp a camp set up for the accommodation of refugees

Taliban a fundamentalist Muslim movement whose militia took control of much of Afghanistan

visa a note in a passport to say that person is allowed to enter, leave, or stay for a specified period of time in a country

USEFUL INFORMATION

Here are some books and websites you might find interesting:

Books

Refugee Boy, by Benjamim Zephaniah, published by Bloomsbury http://benjaminzephaniah.com/books/refugee-boy-3/

Gervelie's Journey, Mohammed's Journey, Hamzat's Journey and *Meltem's Journey*, by Anthony Robinson, Series Editor Annemarie Young. Each book tells, in their own voice, the true story of one refugee child.

The Refugee Diaries series was originally published by Frances Lincoln. New editions published by SpeakOut Publishing: http://www.speakout-publishing.org/#Journeys

Journey to Jo'burg, by Beverley Naidoo, originally published by Collins: http://www.beverleynaidoo.com/JtoJ.htm

Websites

Migration Museum Project:
http://migrationmuseum.org
This project plans to create the UK's first dedicated Migration Museum.

Muzoon Almellehan, (https://www.malala.org). You can watch Muzoon's speech to the Syria Conference: https://www.youtube.com/watch?v=KGm_zcDwnXE

19 Princelet Street: http://19princeletstreet.org.uk is the first museum of immigration and diversity in Europe.

Refugees welcome! Meet the British families who have opened their homes to asylum seekers: http://www.theguardian.com/world/2015/sep/07/british-families-open-homes-asylum-seekers-refugees

This is Exile: diaries of child refugees: https://www.youtube.com/watch?v=AmeZ8PlpJQw. This film is a portrait of child refugees forced to flee from the violence of Syria's civil war to neighbouring Lebanon. It tells the stories of the children's lives in their own words.

Amnesty International is an international organisation that campaigns for human rights throughout the world. It also provides educational resources: https://www.amnesty.org.uk/issues/Education

'What would you do?' on pages 42-43 is based on a role play originally designed by Amnesty.

Project Paddington: http://projectpaddington.com Fund-raising project helping children respond to the refugee crisis, initially by sending their teddy bears to refugee children.

Organisations

International Committee of the Red Cross: https://www.icrc.org

United Nations Human Rights Council – UNHCR: http://www.unhcr.org.uk

Refugee Councils: https://www.refugeecouncil.org.uk / http://www.rcusa.org / http://www.refugeecouncil.org.au /Canadian Council for Refugees: http://ccrweb.ca

Asylum Aid: http://www.asylumaid.org.uk

Joint Council for the Welfare of Immigrants: https://www.jcwi.org.uk

Coram Children's Legal Centre: http://www.childrenslegalcentre.com/index.php?page=migrant_children

Migrants Rights Network: http://www.migrantsrights.org.uk

Migrant Voice: http://www.migrantvoice.org

Refugee Action: http://www.refugee-action.org.uk

Refugee Studies Centre: http://www.rsc.ox.ac.uk

INDEX